For Narnie…………the brightest star

Second edition

My name is Maisie and this is me with my Grandad's dog Kylo. I am all grown up now but not long ago I had a Grandma. I called her Narnie. You might be lucky enough to have a Grandma too, but you may call yours "Granny or Nana" she may be your "Nan or Mommar" but whatever her name is I am sure she is a super star.

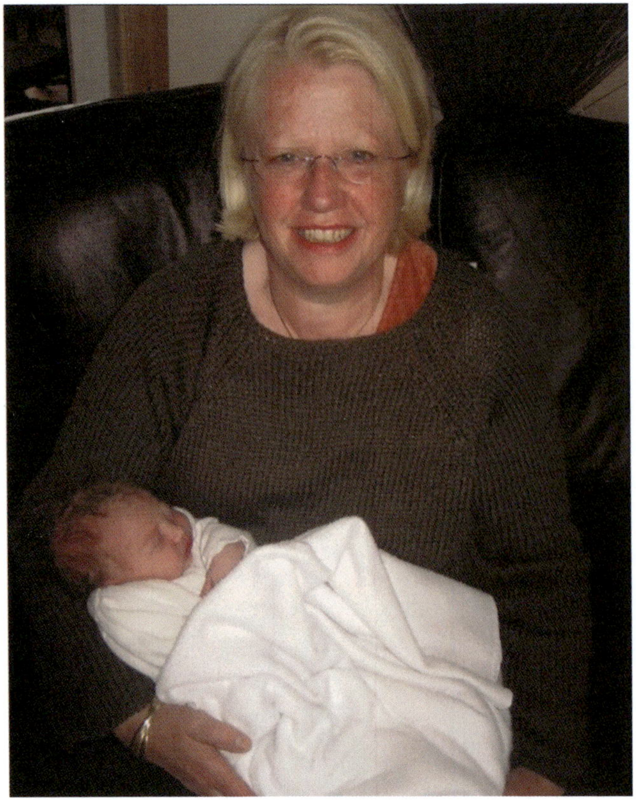

Do you want to know something really special? My Narnie was a super dooper whooper of a star. This is a picture of me and her on the very day that I was born. Look at how happy she was with her huge smile. Look how scrunched up my little face was while I slept cuddled in her arms. My Narnie always gave the very best cuddles.

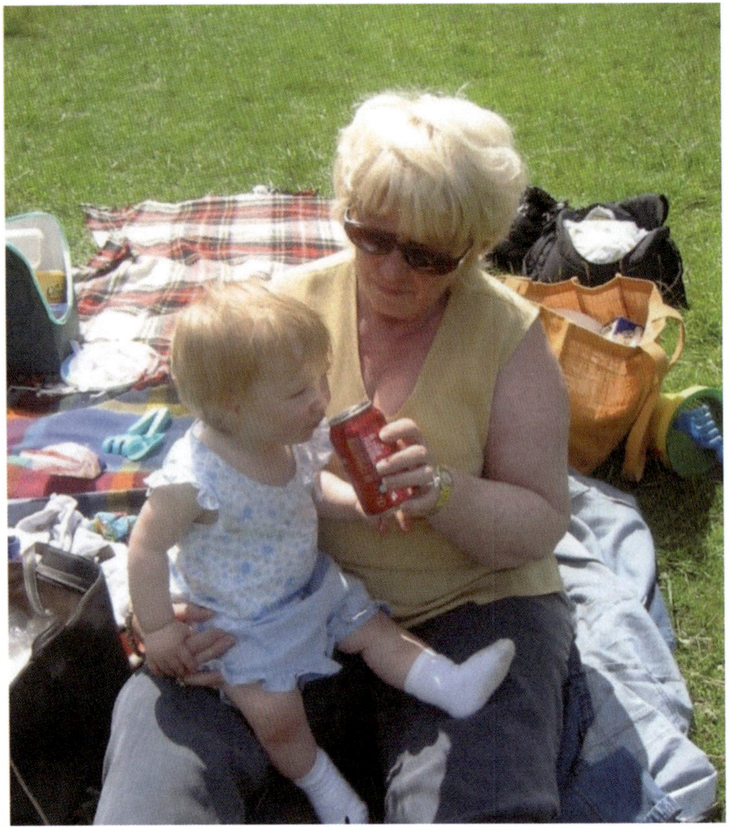

The most wonderful things about Grandmas and Narnies is that they like to spoil you and treat you to things your parents might not let you have. If my mummy said "no" then my Narnie would whisper "yes" and she would give me a wink and her eyes would twinkle and it would be our secret. Here she is letting me taste some of her fizzy drink. "Just a little sip" she would say.

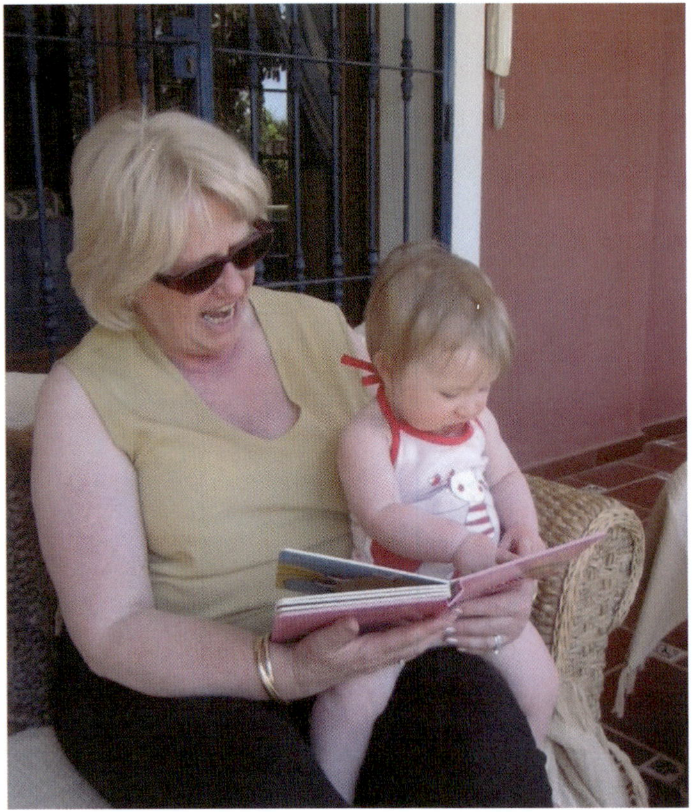

We were best friends from the beginning my Narnie and me. She had a big comfy lap where I would sit and we would sing nursery rhymes and look at picture books together. She would take my tiny feet in her hands "this little piggy went to market, this little piggy stayed at home" she would say. She would place her finger on the palm of my hand "round and round the garden like a teddy bear. 1 step…2 steps…tickle you under there" and she would tickle me and I would giggle.

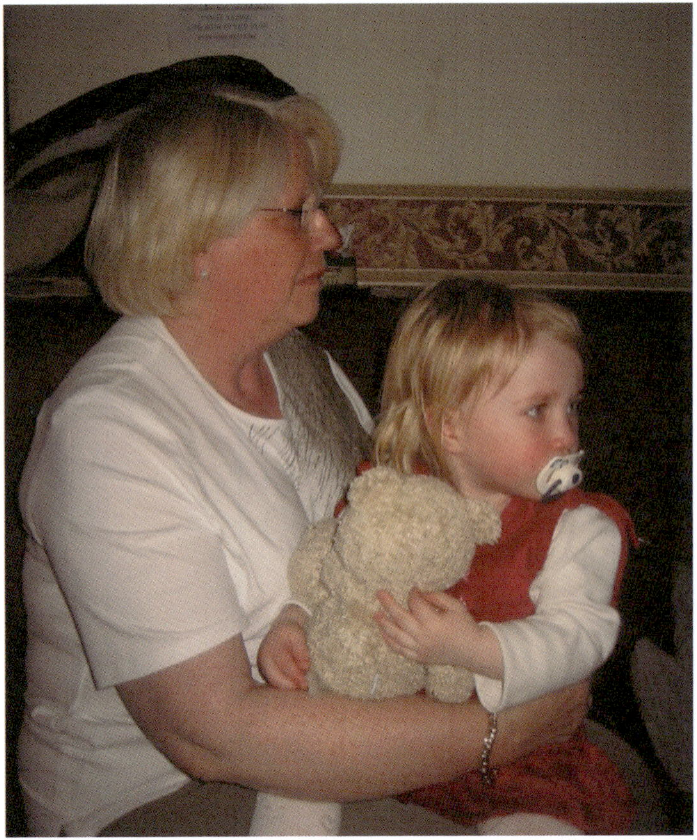

But there were times when I was too tired to play or look at books and those times were my favourite. I would just sit on her big comfy lap and feel so safe and so loved that it did not matter what else was going on around me. I had a big fluffy teddy in those days, I call him Teddy Hiscox. Even though I am all grown up now, Teddy Hiscox still likes to sleep in my bed with me. He is a little more scraggy and baggy now and nowhere near as fluffy but I love him just the same. I had a dummy too (but I gave that up a long time ago).

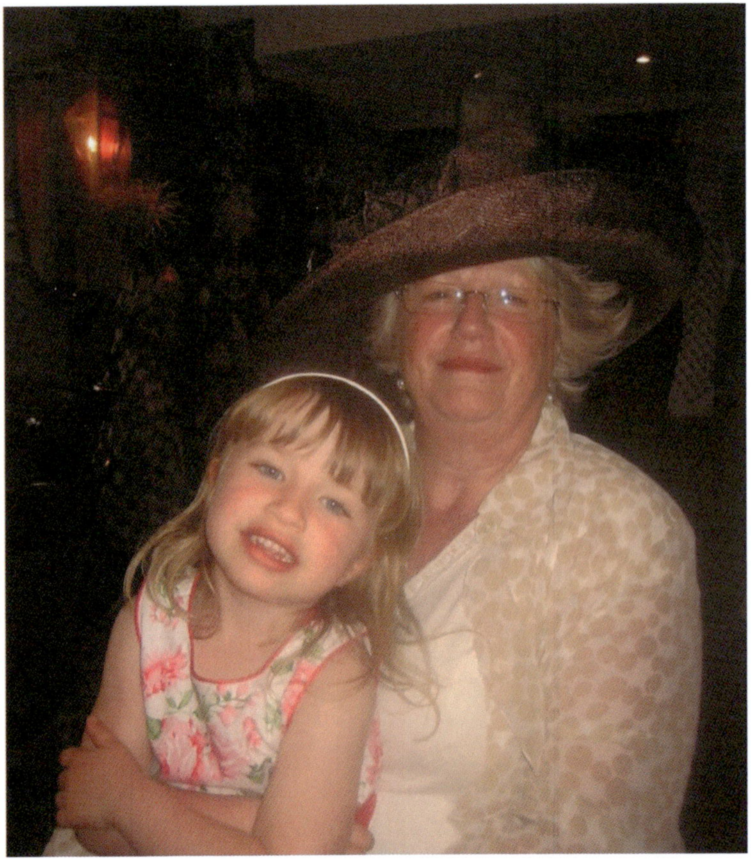

Here we are at a family wedding. My Narnie loved to get all dressed up. She would go to the hairdressers and paint her nails all pretty. She loved parties and gatherings. Doesn't she look beautiful in her lovely hat. My Narnie loved her beautiful clothes and was never happier than when all the family were celebrating together.

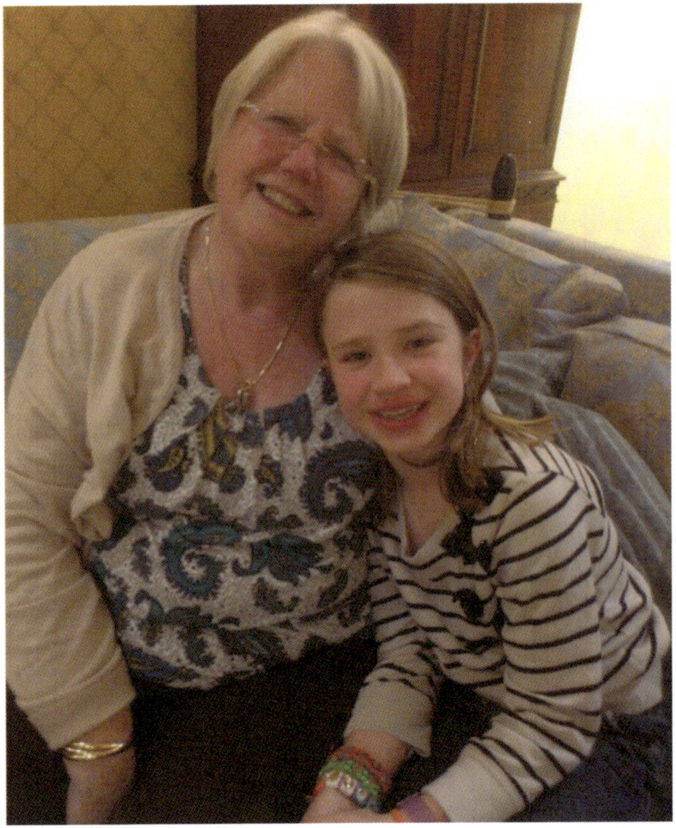

If my mummy ever went out to meet her friends, me and my two brothers would spend the time at Narnie's house. It was always such a treat and we would be even more excited if were able to have a sleep over. We had a bedroom that was decorated like a jungle. There were cuddly parrots and lions on a chair and pictures of animals on the wall. There was even a rug with a zebra print on the floor. We had tiger print covers and there was a bookcase filled with all kinds of books to look at. We all slept in the one room. I would have the single bed and the boys would share the bunk beds. Narnie would sit in the middle of the beds and read us a story. Our favourite was The Owl and the Pussy Cat which she would sing the words to and use a funny voice. Story time with Narnie was such fun and we all loved spending that special time with her all squeezed in one room. A whole room filled with love.

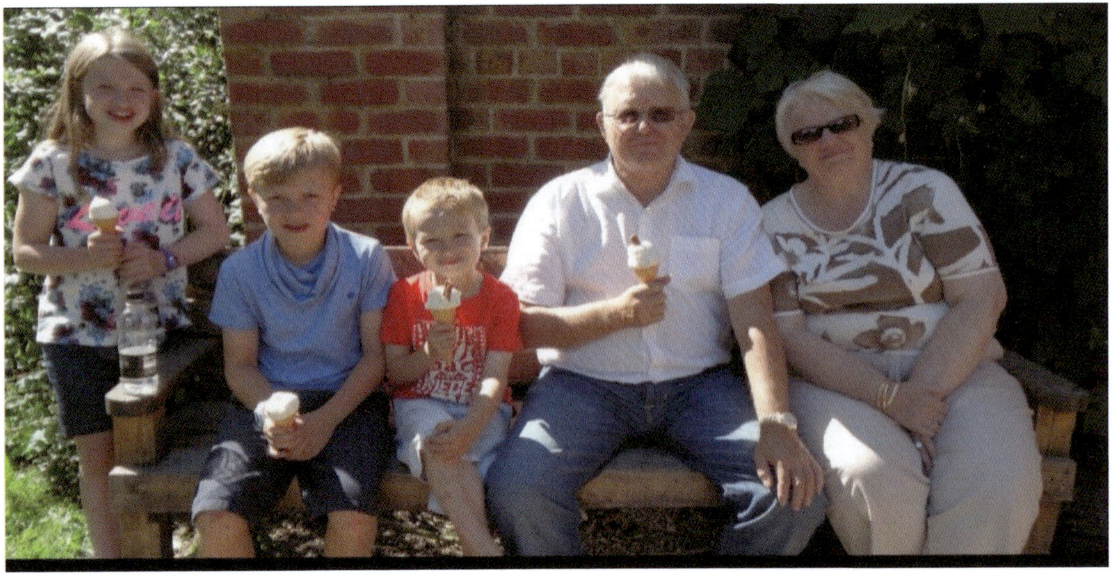

Narnie and Gargan (you might call yours Grandad) used to take us for days out. We went to the farm, to old halls, on drives to the seaside, on steam trains and river boats, to beautiful country gardens or shopping for exciting treats. Wherever we went we usually had an ice cream. Narnie would say "I scream, you scream, we all scream for ice cream". Then we would all laugh as the ice cream melted onto our hands.

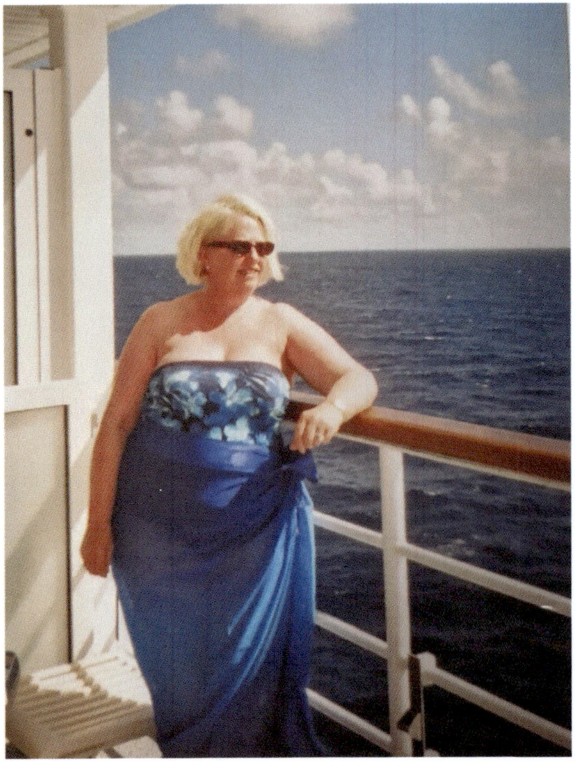

My Narnie loved to go on holiday. She has been to lots and lots of different countries and seen many wonderful places. She told me that one day when the time has come she would float all around the world and see all the things that she has never seen before. I asked her "will you fly with your own wings?" and she said "no, I wont have wings". I wondered would she be a space explorer or a bubble floating around the sky? She told me "I'll be a star, a bright twinkling star"

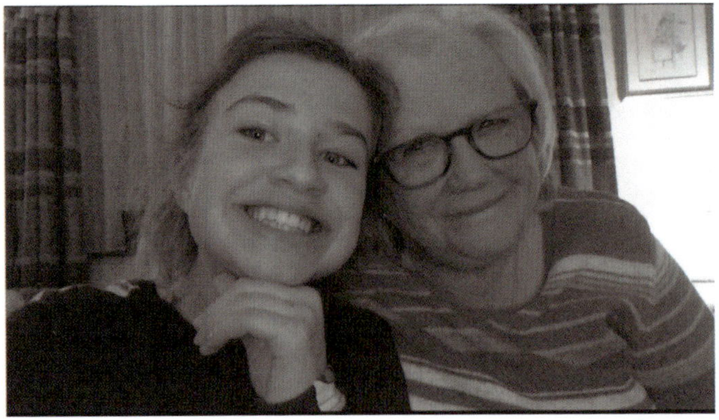

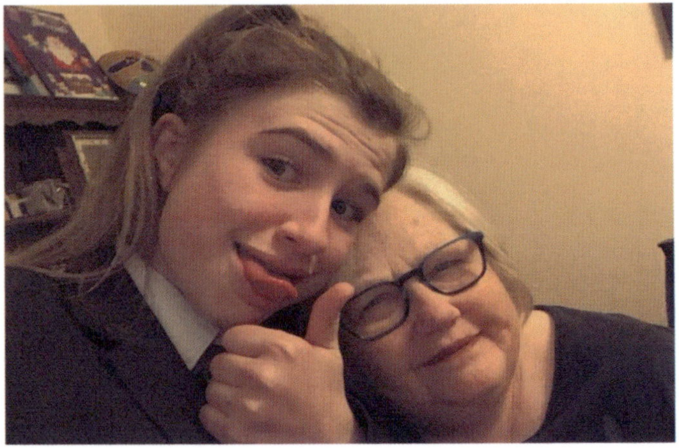

We used to have a lot of photographs taken together. Narnie would say "cheese" and give a huge smile. Her eyes would shine and she would want to have a look at the picture straight away. She would say "send me that one will you?". We took so many silly selfies. My camera roll is full of them and I love every single one. I don't think you can ever have too many photographs. Sometimes it is all you have left.

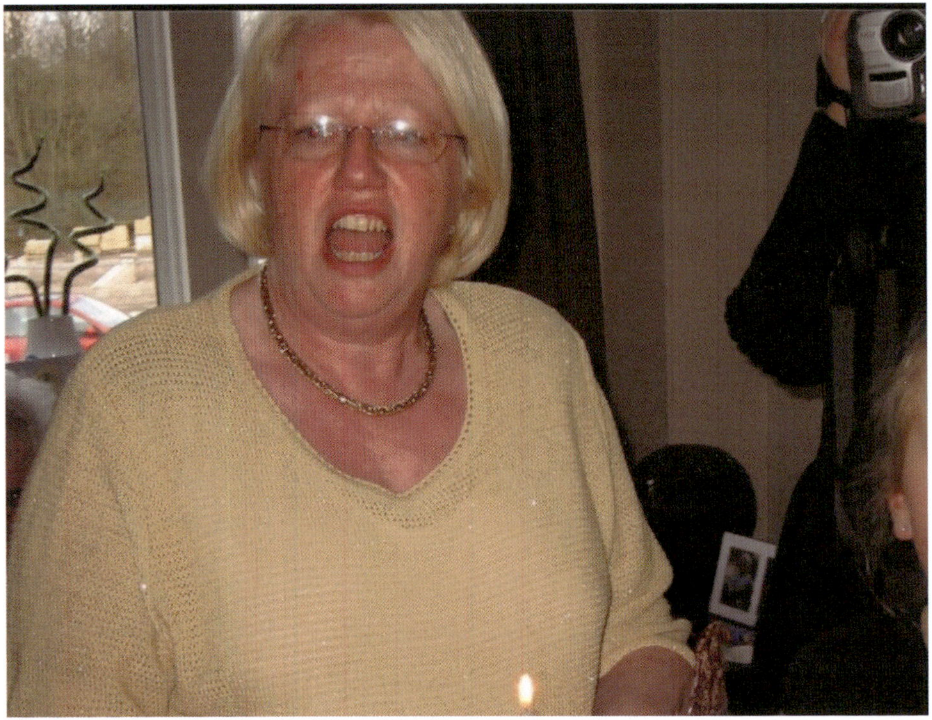

Narnie used to bake. She would bake biscuits and cakes and puddings and pies. She was the best baker ever and I would sometimes help her. She let me add the chocolate chips or mix the ingredients together. She would let me fill the cake tins and bun cases with mixture and make sure I was careful not to stand too close as she popped them in the oven. Then whilst the cakes were baking she would give me the mixing bowl and let me run my finger around the inside to scoop up the mixture and taste it. She would say "who wants to lick the bowl?" and I would squeal "Me! Me!".

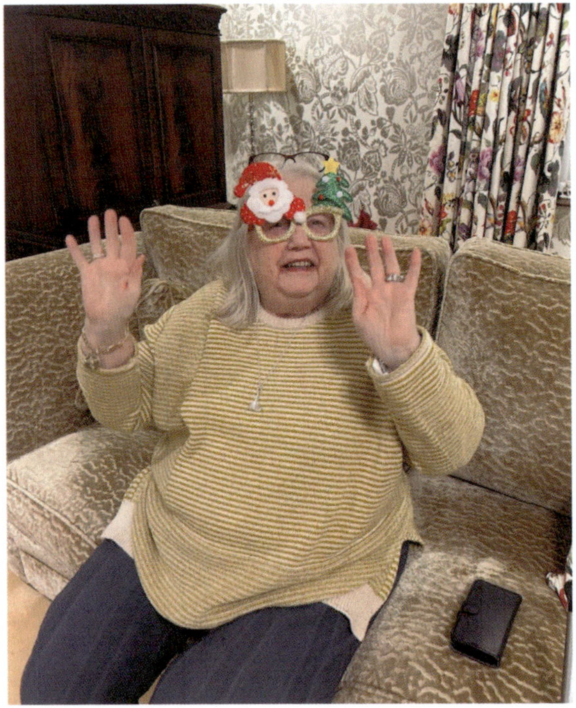

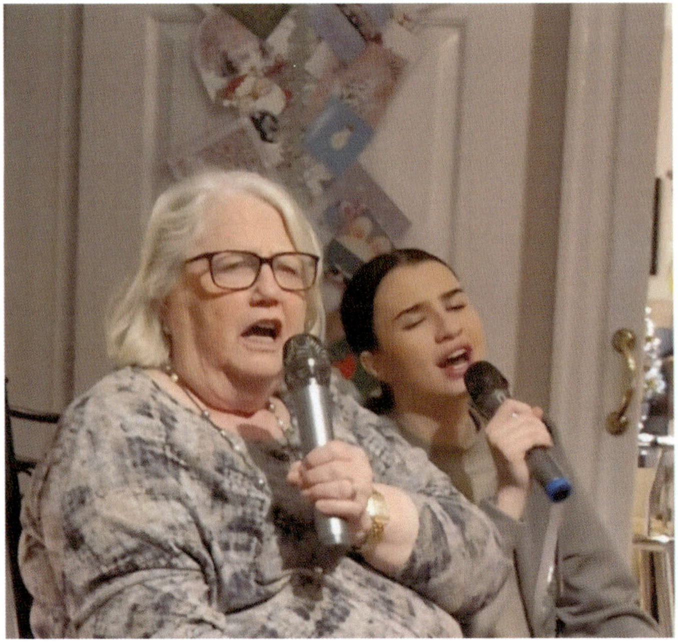

Narnie loved Christmas. It was her favourite time of year. She would write lots of lists. Lists of who to send cards to, who to buy presents for, which delicious food to buy and she would lose her lists and have to start all over again.

She enjoyed singing Christmas songs and decorating her house. Narnie had a beautiful Christmas tree with baubles she had collected over the years. But her favourite part of Christmas was the family parties. She loved to play games and sing.

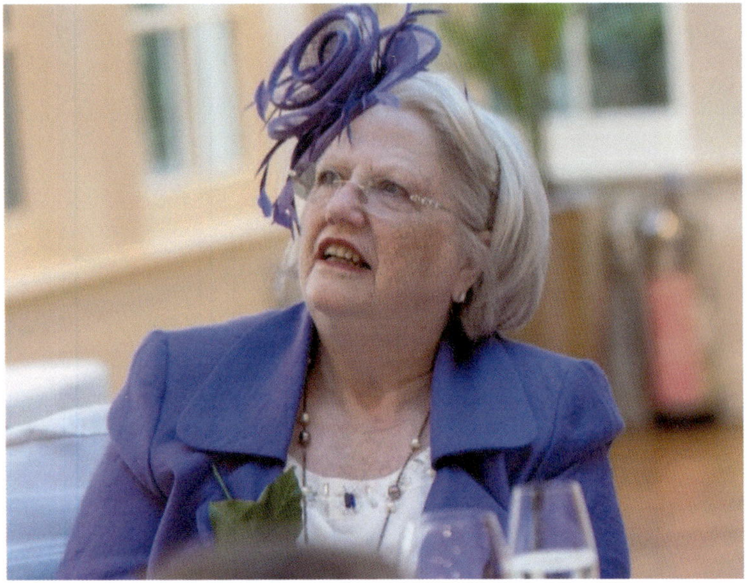

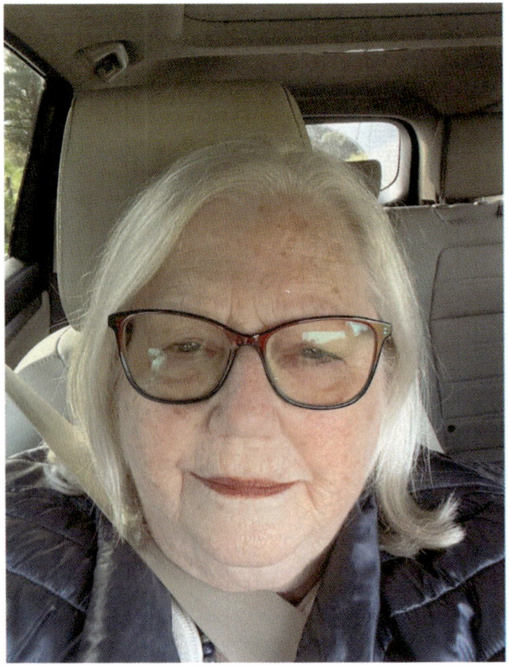

My Narnie was so beautiful. She loved to wear bright colours, hats, scarves and jewellery. She wore pretty make-up on her eyes and cheeks and lipstick on her lips. She would kiss me on my cheek and leave a little lipstick mark. I would rub it off with my fingers and laugh, but I loved it really. If I try hard I can still remember the smell of her perfume.

Here is a picture of my Narnie taking her very own selfie in the car when she had just collected her new glasses.

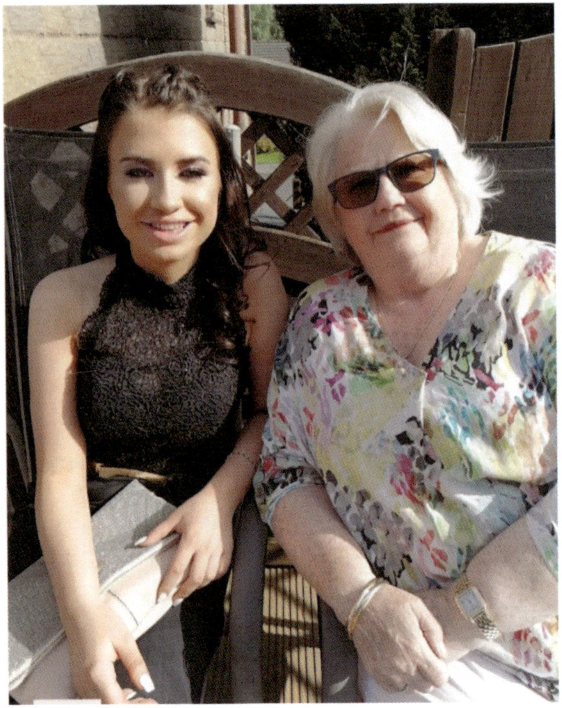

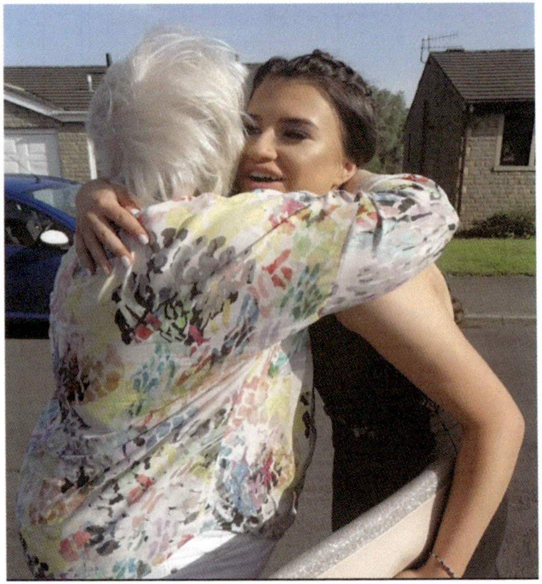

Here I am in my very best clothes. When it was my last day at big school we had a huge party called a Prom. We got dressed up, had our hair done and went to a special restaurant to have a really fancy meal. There was music and dancing and it was such a lovely way to say goodbye to our teachers and friends. My Narnie was excited that I was wearing a dress because she said I did not wear dresses enough. She came to wave at me when I got in the car that took me to the prom.

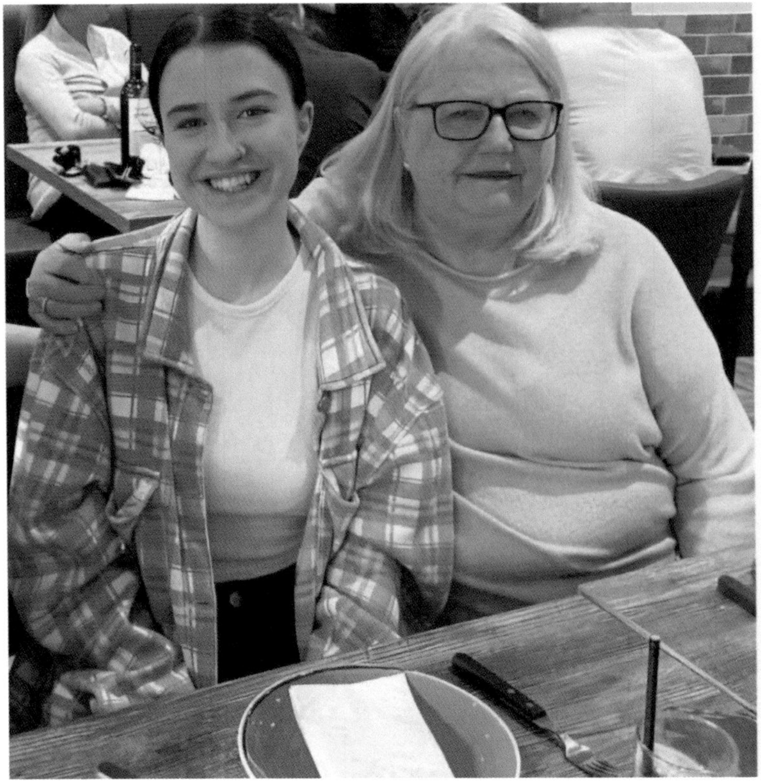

Sometimes when I had some free time Narnie would phone me to see if I wanted to meet up with her to go out for some lunch. She would call it "having a bite to eat". I loved going out for meals with her. She would let me choose anything off the menu. I usually wanted a steak. Then, because my Narnie had a "sweet tooth" we would always have a pudding. These were very special times I shared with her and I treasure them for ever.

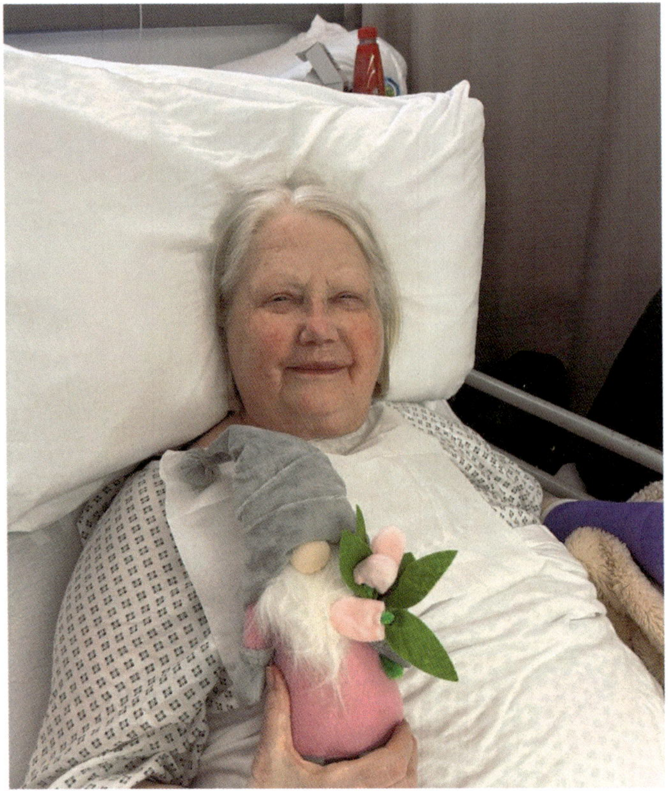

One day my Narnie got poorly. She started to feel a little bit dizzy and she had a sickly tummy. She went to the doctor and they said she needed to go to the hospital. When she was in the hospital she had to stay in bed, but she still had a brave smiling face. She would sing her favourite songs and make the nurses laugh by saying funny things. My Narnie started to get very tired and slept a lot of the time. We all went to see her every day and when it was time for us to go home we told her we would be back tomorrow. We took her nice things to eat and drink because hospital food sometimes is not very nice.

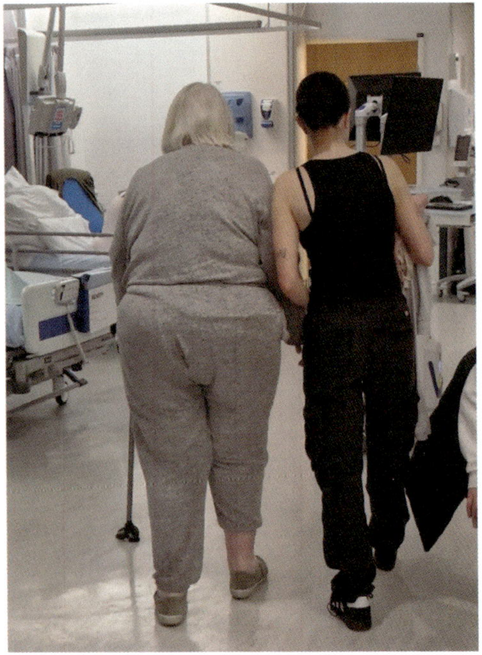

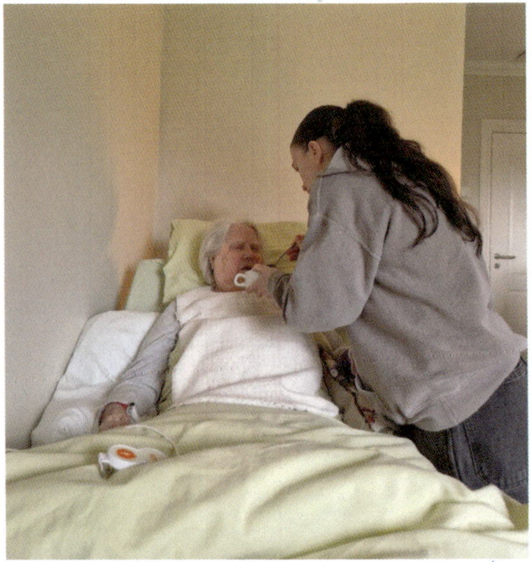

She found it hard to do some things for herself because she was very tired a lot of the time so I helped her. I held her arm as she walked and fed her her food so she did not spill it. It was my turn to look after my Narnie because she had looked after me so well for a long long time. I wanted to make her happy and comfortable and have nothing to worry about. She said "thank you Maisie. I love you babes".

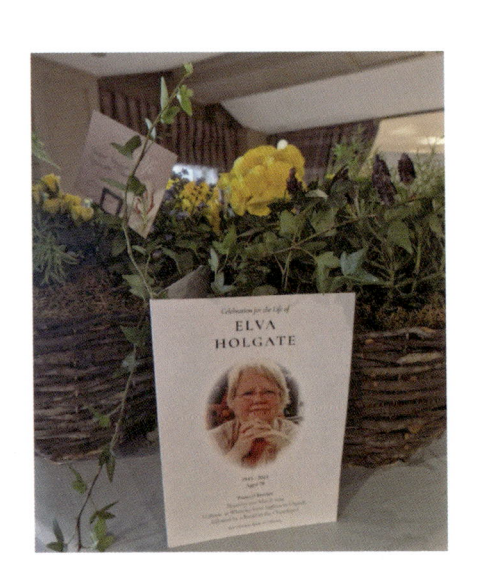

On a very sunny day when my Narnie was sleeping safe in her bed, I knew that the time had come. It was time for her to go and see the world. To see all the things she had never seen before. We had a huge party and invited all her family and friends. We had a really fancy meal. There was music and singing and it was such a lovely way to say goodbye to her.
My narnie was ready to float around the sky with no wings just the way she had told me she would do all those years ago because you see…………………….   my Narnie is a star.

.........love you babes.

Printed in Dunstable, United Kingdom